Fort Knox

Bullion Depository

Written by Julia Hargrove

Illustrated by Gary Mohrman

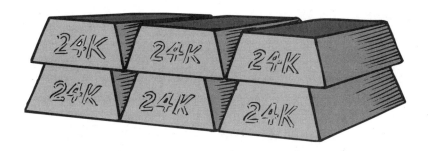

Teaching & Learning Company

1204 Buchanan St., P.O. Box 10
Carthage, IL 62321-0010

This book belongs to

_____

Cover photo by Wesley Treat.
www.wesleytreat.com

Copyright © 2003, Teaching & Learning Company

ISBN No. 1-57310-404-3

Printing No. 987654321

Teaching & Learning Company
1204 Buchanan St., P.O. Box 10
Carthage, IL 62321-0010

Table of Contents

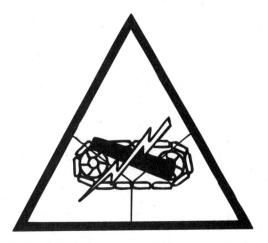

United States Army Training Center

Dear Teacher or Parent,

What is the first thing that comes to your mind when you think of Fort Knox? Stacks of gold bricks? A huge vault of steel and concrete? The movie *Goldfinger*? Yes, all of those things are related to the topic, but Fort Knox is much more than that. It is also a military installation where many cavalry and armored units are stationed and where every person in the army in an armored unit goes to be trained. It is the Patton Museum of Cavalry and Armor where many examples of the world's tanks, armored trucks, LSTs and other armored vehicles are housed. And it is the annual Fourth of July re-enactment of World War II battles between German and U.S. armored vehicles.

Fort Knox has entered our culture and language as no other gold depository in the U.S. has. Most people don't even know where the other four bullion depositories are located, but we've all heard of Fort Knox. As for the language, if your teenager asked you for extra money to buy the latest fashionable shoes, you might reply, "What do you think this is, Fort Knox?"

Some of the United States' most famous landmarks were built in the 1930s. Fort Knox was constructed in 1936-1937. The Empire State Building was erected in 1930-1931. Mount Rushmore was carved from the Black Hills with dynamite throughout the 1930s. And citizens of San Francisco waited from 1933 until 1938 while the Golden Gate Bridge was built and opened to automobile traffic. What amazing vestige of hope in the bleak 1930s caused the flowering of such landmarks? If you would be interested in a unit for your student(s) on the landmarks of the 1930s, the Teaching & Learning Company has a book on Mount Rushmore.

Sincerely,

Julia

Julia Hargrove

Name_____

Fort Knox Bullion Depository[1]

The Fort Knox Bullion Depository in Fort Knox, Kentucky, is one of five places where the United States government stores its gold reserves. (Bullion is gold or silver in the form of bars or sometimes coins.) The other four sites are the Philadelphia Mint, the Denver Mint, the West Point Bullion Depository and the San Francisco Assay Office. All of these places are part of the United States Mint and under the supervision of the Director of the Mint. A mint is a place where coins are made. Some coins used to be made of gold or silver mixed with other metals. This is no longer true in the United States, but the gold reserves still belong to the United States Mint.

The Fort Knox Bullion Depository was built in 1936. The government constructed the Depository on land that formerly belonged to the Fort Knox military reservation. The stronghold for the gold bullion cost $560,000 during the Great Depression. (The cost would be many times that in today's money.) The outside wall of the Depository is made of granite lined with concrete that is reinforced with steel. The finished building is two stories tall and measures 105' x 121' x 42' in height. Construction materials included 16,500 cubic feet of granite, 4200 cubic yards of concrete, 750 tons of reinforcing steel and 670 tons of structural steel. (Structural steel is made into pillars or columns that hold up the building. Reinforcing steel has the concrete poured over it to make the concrete stronger.)

The Bullion Depository at Fort Knox has other means of protecting its precious metals besides the strength of its building materials. The Fort Knox military reservation is one means of protection. There is also a steel fence around the depository. Each corner of the Depository has a manned guard box, and there are two manned sentry boxes at the entry gate. Inside the building are the most modern detection and protection devices. The building is also equipped with its own emergency power generator, water facilities and other services that make it self-sufficient.

The vault inside the granite, concrete and steel building provides yet another layer of protection for the precious metals. The vault is made of steel plates, steel I-beams and steel cylinders covered with concrete. The door to the vault weighs more than 20 tons. Offices and storage areas lie between the vault and the outside walls of the Depository. Therefore, no one could blow up the outside walls of the depository and directly enter the vault. Further security is provided by the fact that no one person knows the entire combination to the vault door: several people have to dial separate combinations that only they know. In addition, the vault cannot be opened except by order of the President of the United States.

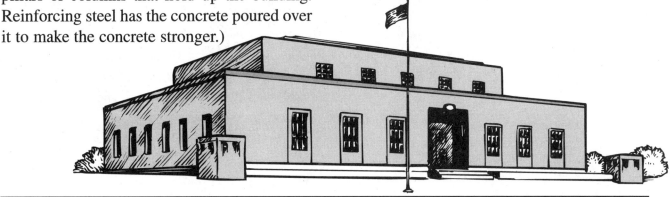

[1]"Fact Sheets: Currency and Coins—Fort Knox Bullion Depository" www.ustreas.gov/education/factsheets/currency/fort-knox.html

Name _____

Fort Knox Bullion Depository

The gold at Fort Knox is stored in the form of bars. These bars are made of almost 100% gold or from gold coins that have been melted down. The bars are about 7" x 3⁵/₈" x 1³/₄" in size—slightly smaller than a brick used in the construction of buildings. Each bar weighs 400 troy ounces. (Troy weight is used specifically to measure gold, silver and precious gems.) Congress has established the price of gold by law in the U.S. at $42.22 per troy ounce. Therefore, each gold bar is worth $16,888. Gold bricks are stored in stacks without any wrappings around them. Since gold is such a soft metal, the bricks have to be handled carefully to prevent their being dented when they are moved.

It is too bad that most of us will never get to see the amazing sight of all that gold stacked up in the Fort Knox Bullion Depository. No visitors are ever allowed into the facility.

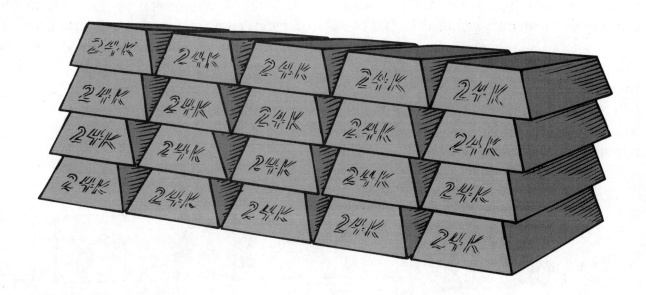

Name_____

Fort Knox Bullion Depository Questions

1. a. Where are the five gold depositories located in the United States? b. What person supervises the

   gold depositories? _____

   _____

2. What is bullion? _____

3. If the price of gold were set at $36 per ounce, what would be the value of a bar of gold?

   _____

4. Troy weight (by which gold is measured) has 12 ounces to a pound. How much does a bar of gold

   weigh in pounds? _____

5. What are both the depository and the vault made of that would make it very difficult to steal the gold

   at Fort Knox? _____

6. What method is used to prevent anyone from learning the combination to the gold vault and stealing

   the gold that way? _____

   _____

7. Thought Question: What are two good reasons for distributing the U.S. gold reserves in five places

   throughout the United States? _____

   _____

8. Historical Research Question: Who was President of the United States when Fort Knox was built?

   _____

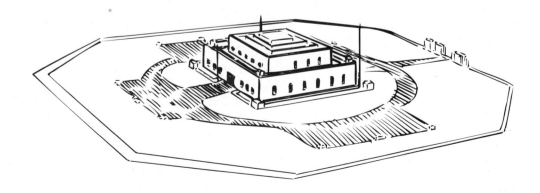

Name _____

Major General Henry Knox[1]

Fort Knox, Kentucky—the military installation and depository for U.S. gold reserves—was named for General Henry Knox, who was a military leader during the Revolutionary War, a friend of George Washington and the United States' first Secretary of War.

William Knox and Mary Campbell Knox came from north Ireland and settled in Boston, Massachusetts. Henry Knox was born in that city in 1750, the seventh of 10 children. William was a shipmaster who traded goods with the West Indies in the Caribbean Sea. However, he died at age 50, leaving Henry to support his mother and siblings. To take care of his family, Henry became a clerk in a bookstore. He later opened a bookstore of his own. This was a good job for Henry because he loved to read about history and artillery. (Artillery is guns too large to carry such as cannons.)

As tensions built between Great Britain and its North American colonies, Henry Knox supported the rebellious colonials. In 1772, he became part of the Boston Grenadier Corps, and he volunteered to fight in the Battle of Bunker Hill in June 1775. That same year, George Washington, commander of the colonial armies, arrived in Boston. General Washington met Knox and asked his advice about driving the British out of Boston. When Knox suggested moving the captured British

cannons from Fort Ticonderoga to Boston, Washington put Knox in charge of the project. The newly commissioned Colonel Knox successfully brought 50 cannons to Boston on ox-drawn sleds. It was the placement of these cannons on Dorchester Heights outside of Boston that drove the British from that city on March 17, 1776.

Washington and Knox next tried to defend New York City from the British, but the Americans were outnumbered 30,000 to 18,000. After retreating from New York, Knox helped Washington capture Trenton and Princeton, New Jersey, over the Christmas and New Year's holidays of 1776-1777. These two victories greatly raised the morale of the colonists, but they were followed by defeats at Brandywine and Germantown, Pennsylvania.

---

[1]"Who Served Here? General Henry Knox"   www.ushistory.org/valleyforge/served/knox.html

Major General Henry Knox

Knox spent part of the winter of 1777-1778 with Washington and his troops at Valley Forge. He helped the German volunteer Baron von Steuben drill and train the troops there. In October 1781, Knox was with Washington at Yorktown, Virginia, the last major battle of the Revolutionary War. Knox's effective placement of his artillery to cut off the British from retreating by land was an important element in the colonial victory over British General Cornwallis. For this service, Knox was promoted to Major General. From 1782 until the peace treaty was signed, Knox was at West Point, New York, helping to defend that strategically important fort.

After the war, Congress—which was the head of the government of the United States under the Articles of Confederation—elected Henry Knox to be Secretary of War in 1785.

Representatives from the states wrote the Constitution in 1787. The new government under the Constitution began in 1789, and President Washington appointed Knox to his cabinet as Secretary of War. Knox served as Secretary until he resigned in 1794 to take care of his large family.

Knox and his family retired to an estate named Montpelier at Thomaston, Maine. Knox's various businesses included manufacturing bricks, raising cattle and building ships. However, he was not a successful businessman and was involved in many lawsuits.[2] He was also active in local government as a member of the General Court and the Governor's Council. He died unexpectedly in 1806 and was buried in Thomaston.

---

[2]*The American Heritage Encyclopedia of American History* edited by John Mack Faragher, New York, Henry Holt and Company, 1998, p. 499.

Name_____

Major General Henry Knox Questions

1. What country did Henry Knox's parents come from? _____

2. What job did Knox take after his father's death in order to support his mother? _____

3. How did Knox get the cannons that he used to surround Boston and drive the British out?

   _____

4. Make two columns on your answer sheet. Write at the top of the first column *Won* and at the top of the second column *Lost*. List under the two columns the battles Knox was involved in that he won and those he fought that he lost.

5. Thought Question: What are two reasons suggested in the text that explain why President Washington

   appointed Henry Knox as his Secretary of War? _____

   _____

6. Thought Question: How would you explain the fact that Knox was talented at military affairs, especially the use of artillery, but was a comparative failure at business and financial affairs?

   _____

   _____

   _____

Fort Knox Military Installation[1]

While the name *Fort Knox* first brings to mind the gold vault there, the fort is also a military post for cavalry and armor units specializing in armor training. Cavalry units used to ride horses, but now they move into battle in tanks. Armor, these days, also refers to tanks or armored trucks. Therefore, the main purpose of Fort Knox is to train soldiers to use tanks and other armored vehicles in battle. There are eight armored units and seven cavalry units at the fort.

Fort Knox is located about 45 miles from Louisville, Kentucky. It is considered to be a city itself, with a daytime population of about 33,000 people. Part of the 109,054 square acres of Fort Knox is next to the Ohio River, which is the northern boundary of the state of Kentucky. The fort covers parts of Bullitt, Hardin and Meade counties. Hardin is one of the oldest counties in Kentucky, having originated when Kentucky became a state in 1792.

The history of the area is interesting. Abraham Lincoln's father, Thomas, owned a small farm on the south end of the fort in the Mill Creek area. Abraham, the future President was born in Hodgenville, which is south of Fort Knox. During the Civil War, both Union and Confederate troops were in this area. The Union Generals Don Carlos Buell and William Tecumseh Sherman occupied Louisville, Kentucky, and land overlooking the Ohio River. The Confederate cavalry leader John Hunt Morgan—who was from Lexington, Kentucky—led raids into what was later to become Fort Knox in 1862. His forces captured several hundred northern troops. Later, Hunt organized a raid into the Northern states of Indiana and Ohio from his base at Brandenburg, Kentucky, west of present-day Fort Knox.

The U.S. government first showed an interest in what is now Fort Knox in 1903 when the Army held training maneuvers there. The United States' entry into World War I in 1917 finally motivated the government to lease 10,000 acres of land near the village of Stithton, Kentucky. The Army established an artillery-training center for soldiers to learn to use long-range guns. The camp was named for Major General Henry Knox, who was the leader of the artillery forces during the Revolutionary War and the U.S.'s first Secretary of War. In July 1918, Congress granted the Army money to buy 40,000 more acres of land in the area. However, the end of the war and the resulting reduction of all military forces meant that the camp closed in 1922. From then until 1932, various military units occasionally used the land for military training.

[1]"Fort Knox"   http://www.globalsecurity.org/military/facility/fort-knox.htm

Fort Knox Military Installation

Fort Knox was revitalized during the Great Depression when the federal government decided to build the U.S. Bullion Depository (or Gold Vault) on the land in 1936. The vault was finished in 1937. That same year, a terrible flooding of the Ohio River overwhelmed Louisville, Kentucky; and the 7th Cavalry Brigade (Mechanized) arrived to help the residents of that city and other nearby communities.

During World War II, the U.S. government moved more and more of its gold reserves to the Gold Vault. While the Germans were bombing England, the British sent the crown jewels and the Magna Carta (a valuable historic document like the U.S. Bill of Rights) to be kept safely at Fort Knox. Some other foreign countries trusted the U.S. to keep their gold reserves during the time that the Germans occupied their nations.

Since World War II, Fort Knox has been "the Home of Mounted Warfare." It has successfully developed military tactics, policies and equipment for armored divisions. It is active in training Army and Army Reserve units in these aspects of armored warfare. Every soldier who serves in an armored unit has been stationed at Fort Knox at least once. The Fort also provides protection for the Gold Vault, and is the site of the Patton Museum of Cavalry and Armor.

Name_____

Fort Knox Military Installation Questions

1. What war caused the U.S. government to buy the land that became Fort Knox? _____

2. When was the U.S. Bullion Depository built at Fort Knox? _____

3. What is the main job of the military installation at Fort Knox?_____

   _____

4. a. What do cavalry units ride now instead of horses? b. Armor divisions in the military fight in what

   kinds of military vehicles? _____

5. Why was Fort Knox closed in 1922? _____

   _____

6. What are two reasons why Fort Knox was re-opened in the 1930s? _____

   _____

   _____

7. What were two reasons why England and some other foreign countries stored their valuables and gold

   in the U.S. Gold Vault at Fort Knox? _____

   _____

8. Historical Research Question: Look at a map of the United States during the Civil War. Explain why

   both Union and Confederate troops would have sent troops through Kentucky. _____

   _____

   _____

Name_____

Fort Knox—Reading a Chart[1]

Write your answers on your own sheet of paper unless your teacher tells you otherwise. All *explanations* must be written in complete sentences in order to express a complete thought.

1. First, read the information at the top of the chart.

   a. What are the three topics about which the chart shows information?

   b. Notice that the dates for the information are given by fiscal year. (See first column.) A fiscal year is an accounting year, a year during which an organization keeps track of its money. A fiscal year can begin at any time during a calendar year. For instance, some organizations' fiscal years run from July 1 through June 30. If Fort Knox's fiscal year ends September 30, on what date does the new fiscal year begin?

   c. Notice that the *Expenditures* heading has "($000)" beside it. That means that the dollar amounts are shown in thousands. In other words, three zeros have been left off all of the numbers shown in the expenditures columns (probably to save space on the chart). Knowing this, show the total amount of money Fort Knox spent in 1984. (Remember: In all of your answers about money based on this chart, you must add those three zeros to the answers.)

   d. Look at the bottom of the chart. i. What is the source of the information on the chart? ii. Why is it important to know the source of information?

   e. Look at the *Payroll* column under *Expenditures* i. Information in that column includes wages for active duty personnel, civilian employees and what other group of people? ii. Is there any place on the chart that shows how many people are in that third group? If so, tell how many of those people are being paid by Fort Knox.

   f. What is the difference between *Active Duty Personnel* and *Civilian Employees*? In order to tell the difference between two things, you must describe both of them.

   g. The last column under *Civilian Employees* is headed *DOD Other*. Look at the source at the bottom of the page and explain what *DOD* stands for.

   h. For what years does this chart give financial (money) information about Fort Knox?

2. What is the first year that the Navy hired civilian employees to work at Fort Knox?

3. a. How much more money did Fort Knox spend in fiscal year 1991 than it did in fiscal year 1992? b. How is that reduction in expenditures reflected in the *Prime Contracts* column? c. What would you expect the numbers under *Total Personnel* do to reflect the decrease in expenditures? Show the figures for 1991 and 1992 *Total Personnel* to prove that your guess was correct.

4. What was the average number of Air Force employees at Fort Knox during the 15 years shown on the chart? (To find the average, add up the number of employees for each year. Then divide the total number of employees by the total number of years—15. The five years when there were no Air Force employees at Fort Knox goes into the average. That is accomplished when you divide by 15 years instead of 10 years.)

5. a. In what year did Fort Knox spend the highest amount of money for Prime Contracts, and how much was spent that year? b. Thought Question: Why do you suppose the amount spent on Prime Contracts varied so much from year to year?

6. Thought Question: A military installation like Fort Knox generates money for the city near which it is located. a. What is one way the military men and women at Fort Knox might put money into the city's economy? b. What is one way the civilian employees might put money into the city's economy?

[1]"Fort Knox"   http://www.state.ky.us/agencies/kcma/assets/page18.htm

Fort Knox—Reading a Chart

| Fiscal Year ending Sept 30 | Expenditures ($000) | | | Total Personnel | Active Duty Personnel | | | | Civilian Employees | | | | |
	Total	Payroll (incl. est. of retirement pay)	Prime Contracts		Total	Army	Navy	Air Force	Total	Army	Navy	Air Force	DOD Other
1984	$458,571	$396,419	$62,125	21,985	17,451	17,395	20	36	4,534	4,509		1	24
1985	$487,651	$404,126	$83,525	22,824	17,546	17,489	22	35	5,278	5,254		1	23
1986	$494,184	$394,521	$99,663	22,699	17,739	17,687	22	30	4,960	4,936		1	23
1987	$526,487	$437,869	$88,618	22,022	17,012	16,961	15	36	5,010	4,982		1	27
1988	$476,277	$414,207	$62,070	20,611	16,019	15,846	140	33	4,592	4,569			23
1989	$673,022	$606,831	$66,191	22,075	17,071	16,933	13	35	5,004	4,981			23
1990	$349,526	$278,200	$71,326	15,920	11,698	11,508	155	35	4,222	4,201			21
1991	$630,741	$522,332	$108,409	17,661	13,073	12,897	140	36	4,588	3,861			727
1992	$614,603	$521,191	$93,412	16,607	11,843	11,688	112	43	4,764	3,856	38		870
1993	$623,616	$528,955	$94,661	16,134	11,693	11,538	116	39	4,441	3,533	30	1	877
1994	$629,217	$518,675	$110,542	15,985	11,528	11,340	150	38	4,457	3,528	19	1	909
1995	$524,807	$427,726	$97,081	12,819	8,455	8,281	153	21	4,364	3,507	8	3	839
1996	$588,099	$443,837	$144,262	14,297	9,990	9,854	127	18	4,307	3,454	15	1	837
1997	$460,489	$360,982	$99,507	14,522	10,251	10,084	146	21	4,080	3,342	3	1	734
1998	$556,445	$467,725	$88,720	14,294	10,546	10,385	146	15	3,748	3,061		1	686

Source: *Atlas/Data Abstract for the United States and Selected Areas,* Department of Defense, Washington Headquarters Services, Directorate for Information, Operations and Reports (DIOR), various years.

Patton Museum of Cavalry and Armor

Fort Knox, Kentucky

General George S. Patton[1]

General Patton, for whom the armor museum at Fort Knox is named, is one of the most famous generals of World War II. When Patton went to West Point in the early 1900s, *cavalry* meant "horse-mounted troops"; but he quickly adapted to cavalry as armored vehicles during World War I and was a tank commander in World War II.

In 1942 during the Second World War, Patton first fought in North Africa against German General Rommel's Afrika Korps. The U.S. and British Allies drove the Germans out of Africa. Then Patton captured Sicily, which was the first step to the invasion of Italy. Because of a controversial incident in which Patton slapped a soldier for supposedly being a coward, the general did not participate in the D-Day invasion of Normandy, France. However, with the huge German counterattack called the Battle of the Bulge, Patton was given a second chance and command of the new Third Army. His most spectacular achievement during this campaign was the relief of Bastogne, which was surrounded by Germans, in December 1944. Patton then participated in the conquest of Germany by taking his troops into Bavaria.

Patton died as the result of an automobile accident in December 1945, only seven months after the war in Europe ended. Among the items at the Patton Museum are the general's ivory-handled revolvers, his 2$\frac{1}{2}$-ton command truck and the automobile that was involved in his fatal accident.

[1]*The American Heritage Encyclopedia of American History* edited by John Mack Faragher, New York, Henry Holt and Company, 1998.

Patton Museum of Cavalry and Armor
Fort Knox, Kentucky

Patton Museum of Cavalry and Armor[2]

The museum is on the Fort Knox military reservation near the Chaffee Street gate onto the base. Because of the terrorist acts of September 11, 2001, security is high at the military base and again at the museum itself. Visitors who are U.S. citizens must have a photo I.D. Foreign-born visitors must show their passports. All visitors are searched for weapons or anything resembling a weapon such as a pocketknife or other sharp objects. People who disobey the rules can be refused entry to the base or the museum.

The museum contains examples of all types of armored vehicles including tanks, self-propelled guns, armored cars and trucks, and World War II LSTs (Landing Ship, Tanks). Some of the vehicles are housed in the museum; some are displayed on the grounds in the open; and others are in storage areas that might require special permission to visit. The museum includes in its collection not only U.S. armored vehicles, but also some examples from other countries such as Israel, Germany, Iraq and Britain. One of the highlights of the museum is the largest tank ever built in the U.S., the *T28 Super Heavy Tank*. The Patton gallery and an excellent library on armored vehicles are two other special features of the museum. Check the museum's web site for information about hours, special requirements for admission to parts of the museum and what to see.

---

[2]"Patton Museum of Cavalry and Armor, Fort Knox, Kentucky" http://ipmslondon.tripos.com/museumreviews/id12.html

Name_____

Patton Museum of Cavalry and Armor Questions

1. When did General Patton have to change his concept of *cavalry* as horse-mounted troops to cavalry as armored vehicles? _____

   _____

2. Give two examples from the text that show that Patton was successful in using tanks and other armored vehicles in battle._____

   _____

3. Thought Question: Why do you suppose the Patton Museum of Cavalry and Armor is named for General Patton and has some of his personal items in its collection? _____

   _____

4. What are two rules that visitors to the base and the Patton Museum have to obey? _____

   _____

   _____

5. Give four examples of types of armored vehicles from the description of the museum.

   _____

   _____

6. Thought Question: What are two reasons why a person might want to visit the Patton Museum of Cavalry and Armor? _____

   _____

Alexander Hamilton— First Secretary of the Treasury

When Alexander Hamilton became the first Secretary of the Treasury under the Constitution, the United States faced many problems. The new nation owed $54 million to private citizens and foreign nations. The people had little confidence in the federal government's ability to repay its debts, so government bonds were worth only 10 or 15 percent of their face value. Under the Articles of Confederation, the national government had had no method of raising money from the states, so Hamilton had to create sources of income for the government under the Constitution. Hamilton's plan to solve these and other problems was to pay off the national debt, pay off the states' debts, put an excise tax on luxury goods, apply a small tariff to imported products, create a National Bank and reform the national currency.

Hamilton's first step was to promise to pay off the national debt at face value and to pay all back interest on the debt. The Secretary of the Treasury could have cheated U.S. creditors by not repaying the loan, or not repaying the full interest on the loans, or repaying the loans at reduced market value rather than full face value. However, Hamilton knew that, if he did not repay the loans at full value with interest, citizens would not buy government bonds and nations would be very reluctant to loan money to the U.S. in the future. He wanted to bind the wealthy people with loyalty to the new government, and the best way to do that was to repay their loans (government bonds) and keep them financially happy.

The second plank in Hamilton's plan was to assume the states' debts, which totaled about $21.5 million. He had two reasons for doing this. First, the states' debts were largely caused by raising money to fight the Revolutionary War. It was right that the federal government should take on this debt because the whole nation had benefited from these debts by winning its independence. Second, Hamilton wanted to gain the loyalty of the states to the new federal government, and one way to do that was to relieve them of their debts. However, this plan set up a conflict between the Southern states and the Northern states. Most of the Southern states either had small debts or had paid off their debt. Many of the Northern states still had large debts. The Southern states didn't think it was fair to have paid their own debts and now have to pay those of the Northern states, too. In the Assumption Bill, Hamilton created a compromise. The Southern states agreed to allow the federal government to take on the states' debts in return for having the nation's new capital city—Washington, D.C.—located in the South between Maryland and Virginia. The Assumption Bill became law in 1790.

---

[1]*The American Pageant* (11th ed.) by Thomas A. Bailey, David M. Kennedy and Lizabeth Cohen, Boston, Massachusetts, Houghton Mifflin Company, 1998.

Alexander Hamilton—
First Secretary of the Treasury

How did Hamilton propose to repay what was now a $75 million debt? Hamilton's plan had three sources of revenue (income): a tariff on imported goods, an excise tax in the U.S. on luxury items and miscellaneous fees and taxes. The tariff was a relatively low 8% tax on the value of taxable products that came into the U.S. from foreign countries. It was up to Congress to decide what foreign goods (imports) would be taxed. The tariff had two advantages. It gave the federal government money to pay off the debt. It also protected U.S. factories by making the prices of foreign goods higher than the prices of U.S. goods so that people in the U.S. were more likely to buy domestic (made in the U.S.) products. The excise tax was put on things made in the U.S. and was usually applied to luxury items. It gave the federal government a source of income, but it also gave it a headache in the form of the Whiskey Rebellion in southwestern Pennsylvania. But George Washington, himself, met with the rebels and resolved that problem. The U.S. now had its sources of income secured.

Finally, Hamilton's plan called for a National Bank to hold the Treasury's money. The U.S. government would be the major stockholder in the Bank, so it would control how the institution was run. Private citizens could also buy stocks in the Bank, giving them income and another reason to be loyal to the new government. The Bank would loan money to states and businesses, which would keep the money in circulation, earn further income for the federal government in the form of interest on the loans and encourage growth and development in the U.S. However, there were serious doubts in Washington's cabinet and in Congress about whether the Bank was constitutional. The Constitution did not say anywhere that Congress had the power to create a bank. On the other hand, Hamilton argued, it did say that Congress had the right to make laws that were "necessary and proper" to carrying out its specific powers. Hamilton won the argument, and Congress chartered the National Bank for 20 years in 1791.

The Secretary of the Treasury also created a new system of money. The previous currency under the Articles of Confederation and the Continental Congress was so corrupted by inflation that it was "not worth a continental" in the slang of the day. The new money was to be based on the decimal system (unlike the old British system). Therefore, 10 dimes would equal a dollar—the value of one dime being 10% of the value of a dollar. One hundred pennies would equal a dollar—the value of one penny being 1% of the value of a dollar. We still use the same system of currency today.

Alexander Hamilton was a brilliant Secretary of the Treasury who put the United States on a sound financial footing that greatly benefited the new nation.

Name_____

Alexander Hamilton—
First Secretary of the Treasury Questions

1. What were the three sources of debt that Hamilton proposed the federal government should pay off?

   _____

2. What were the three sources of revenue (income) Hamilton set up for the federal government?

   _____

3. Give two reasons why Hamilton thought it was important to pay off the national debt.

   _____

   _____

4. What were two reasons why Hamilton thought it was important for the federal government to take over the states' debts and pay them off? _____

   _____

5. What compromise did Hamilton propose in the Assumption Bill so that the Southern states would agree to the federal government's paying off the states' debts? _____

   _____

6. a. What was the major argument against the National Bank? b. What was the major argument for the National Bank? _____

   _____

7. What are three ways in which the National Bank would benefit the citizens of the U.S. and the nation as a whole? _____

   _____

8. a. The value of a quarter in U.S. currency is what fraction of the value of a dollar? b. The value of a quarter is what percent of the value of a dollar? c. Express the percentage of a quarter's value in relation to the dollar as a decimal. _____

9. Thought Question: The argument over the creation of the National Bank is the classic debate between those who want to expand the powers of the federal government and those who want to limit its powers. Write a paragraph of at least six sentences explaining which side you favor and the logical and factual reasons for your answer.

A History of the United States' Banking System[1]

1775-1783—
Revolutionary War

The Continental Congress prints paper money (called "continentals") with almost nothing to back its value. Inflation during the war reduces the value of the money until it is nearly worthless or "not worth a continental."

1777-1787—
Articles of Confederation

A weak central government under the Articles makes it impossible for the Congress to raise money from the states, regulate trade with foreign countries, regulate trade between the states, tax private citizens or control the nation's money and banking. There is no president, either.

1789——Constitution

Government begins under the Constitution with George Washington as President. He appoints Alexander Hamilton as the first Secretary of the Treasury.

1791

Congress passes the law creating the First Bank of the United States. Alexander Hamilton proposes the bank to help distribute and regulate money in the U.S. The National Bank helps control unsound smaller banks, reduces the number of bank failures, issues sound bank notes, promotes economic expansion through loans and keeps U.S. funds stored safely.[2]

1811

The 20-year charter of the National Bank runs out, and Congress refuses to renew it.

1816

Congress passes the charter for the Second Bank of the United States.

1829-1837

President Andrew Jackson opposes the Second Bank of the U.S. as a monopoly that is unfair to farmers, the South and the West. (Jackson considers himself to be a Westerner and a man of the people.) Jackson sets out to destroy the Bank. He takes money out of the National Bank and deposits it in Western banks that became known as "pet banks."[3]

---

[1]"U.S. Banking and the Federal Reserve—A Time Line" www.kc.frb.org/fed101/history/print.htm

[2]*The American Pageant* (11th ed.) by Thomas A. Bailey, David M. Kennedy and Lizabeth Cohen, Boston, Massachusetts, Houghton Mifflin Company, 1998, p. 278.

[3]*Ibid.*, pp. 276-279.

A History of the United States' Banking System

1836

Congress does not renew the charter of the Second Bank of the United States. There is now no central agency to regulate banking and currency or to safely store the federal government's funds.

1836-1865

This period was the so-called free banking era. Without a national banking system, state-chartered banks and unchartered "free banks" were the only places to store money, distribute money and provide loans. These banks also issued their own bank notes, which were not always backed by anything of value.

1863

The National Banking Act creates nationally charted banks. Notes issued by these banks have to be backed by U.S. government securities. The act is later amended to tax notes issued by state banks but not tax notes issued by nationally chartered banks. This has the effect of creating a uniform national currency.

1893

A run on the banks, in which people try to withdraw all of their money at once to make sure it is safe, causes a panic that turns into the worst depression the U.S. has endured in its history. J.P. Morgan and a group of bankers help restore confidence in the nation's banks by loaning the federal government $65 million in gold, charging $7 million in interest.[4]

1907

Speculation on Wall Street in the stock market is a failure and sets off another bank panic (or run on the banks). Another severe depression threatens until financier J.P. Morgan again agrees to bail out the government by loaning it money.

1913

The Federal Reserve Act becomes law on December 23, 1913.

1914

The Federal Reserve Banks in 12 cities throughout the United States begin their work.

[4]*Ibid.*, p. 630.

A History of the United States' Banking System

1929—
Stock Market Crash

Speculation on Wall Street and the practice of artificially raising the price of stocks leads to the stock market crash in October 1929.

1929-1940—
Great Depression

Between 1930 and 1933, ten thousand banks fail in the U.S. and many people lose all the money they had put in the banks. This led to the Great Depression, which remains to this day as the worst depression in U.S. history. The depression eventually spreads worldwide.

1933

President Franklin Roosevelt takes office and begins wide reforms meant to help the people and reform the economic system.

The Banking Act of 1933 (also known as the Glass-Steagall Act) requires the separation of commercial and investment banking. It also says that government securities must be used to back Federal Reserve notes.

The Banking Act also creates the Federal Deposit Insurance Corporation. Under this plan, citizens who lose money in bank failures will be repaid the amount they lost (up to $5000) by the federal government.

Roosevelt takes the United States off the gold standard. (Being on the gold standard means that paper currency can be turned in to the U.S. Treasury in exchange for the face amount of the currency in gold.) He does this by calling in all the gold certificates. The President also has the Treasury raise the price of gold from $21 per ounce to $35 per ounce. No more gold coins are minted after this.

1934

Congress creates the Securities and Exchange Commission to regulate trading on the U.S. stock market.

1951

Federal Reserve Chairman William McChesney Martin sets the precedent of operating separately from the Treasury Department in setting monetary policy.

1956

The Bank Holding Company Act requires that the Federal Reserve Board regulate bank holding companies that own more than one bank.

A History of the United States' Banking System

1970s

Rising oil prices causes inflation and increases the cost of consumer goods. The national deficit more than doubles.

1978

The Humphrey-Hawkins Act makes it a law that the chairman of the Federal Reserve Board has to make a report to Congress twice a year on its monetary policies.

1980s

Federal Reserve Chairman Paul Volker uses policies that successfully control inflation.

1987

October 19, 1987, the stock market crashes. The chairman of the Federal Reserve Board, Alan Greenspan issues a statement that the Federal Reserve is ready to support the nation's economy. This economic policy averts financial failure.

1990s

Alan Greenspan continues as chairman of the Federal Reserve Board throughout this decade. The '90s are marked by declining inflation and the longest peacetime economic expansion in the history of the United States.

1999

Congress passes the Gramm-Leach-Bailey Act that ends the changes made by the Glass-Steagall Act of 1933. Banks can now provide services beyond checking and savings accounts including investment banking and insurance sales.

2000

A dramatic decline in the value of stocks on the stock market begins. Many people's savings and retirement funds are nearly wiped out. This decline presents a great challenge to the Federal Reserve Board and the U.S. economy.

Name_____

A History of the United States' Banking System
Questions

1. What was the name of the first national institution that kept U.S. government money safe and helped to regulate the economy? _____

2. When did the three worst depressions on this time line occur? _____

3. When did the longest period of peacetime economic expansion in the U.S. occur? _____

4. Was Paul Volker a successful or unsuccessful chairman of the Federal Reserve Board? Give evidence from the time line to support your answer._____

   _____

5. What was the only effort between the death of the Second National Bank in 1836 and the creation of the Federal Reserve Board in 1913-1914 to take national control of banking and currency?

   _____

   _____

6. In general, is the period from 1913 to 1954 marked by greater federal control of the economy by the national government or less federal control of the economy? Give proof from the time line to support

   your answer. _____

   _____

   _____

   _____

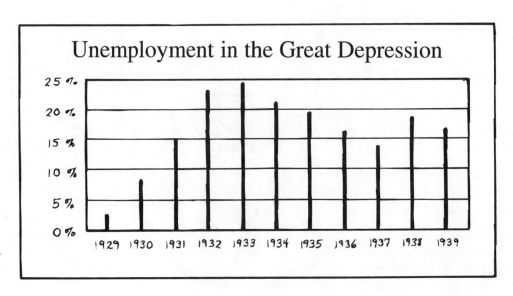

Unemployment in the Great Depression

Introduction to the "Cross of Gold" Speech

The Gold Standard and Bimetallism[1]

The gold standard is a system of money in which, in the United States, the value of the dollar is determined by a fixed amount of gold. The U.S. in 1792 began on a system based on both silver and gold. The relative value of the two metals was set at 15 to 1; in other words, the value of 15 ounces of silver was equal to the value of one ounce of gold. The relative value of both metals changed over time so that people sometimes held onto gold when it was more valuable and sometimes hoarded silver when it was more valuable. The Coinage Act of 1873 ended the minting of silver coins. The U.S. was officially on the gold standard.

The discovery of the Comstock Lode in 1859, along with the discovery of other silver mines in the late 1800s, meant that a great deal of silver was available to be minted into money. Poor people, particularly farmers and factory workers, wanted the free coinage of silver along with the minting of gold coins. The reason they wanted bimetallism (the minting of both silver and gold coins) was to bring down the value of money and make it easier to pay their debts. It works this way. (1) Minting silver coins means more money is in circulation. (2) More money in circulation creates inflation. (3) During a period of inflation, the value of money decreases. (4) The farmer or factory worker could then repay a loan with money that was worth less than the value of the original loan. A $1000 loan would be repaid with $1000 in the face value of coins or paper money, but the value of the $1000 would have been eroded by inflation. Needless to say, the wealthy people who had loaned the money to the farmer or factory worker, did not want to be repaid in devalued money, so they resisted bimetallism and the free coinage of silver.

---

[1]*The American Heritage Encyclopedia of American History* edited by John Mack Faragher, New York, Henry Holt and Company, 1998, pp. 360-361.

Introduction to the "Cross of Gold" Speech

In 1890, Congress passed the Sherman Silver Purchase Act. This provided for the coinage of some silver, but Congress repealed (took back) the law in 1893. This was one of the causes of the terrible depression of 1893.

William Jennings Bryan entered the national political scene in 1890 when he was elected to Congress. He was born in Nebraska in 1860 and stood up politically for the farmer and other poor people. Part of his championing of the farmer was his belief in the coinage of silver at the ratio of 16 to 1 to the value of gold. Bryan made his "Cross of Gold" speech in favor of bimetallism at the Democratic National Convention in 1896. The convention immediately nominated Bryan as its presidential candidate for that year. Bryan lost the election, and the "silverites" lost their campaign for "cheap money" four years later when the Gold Standard Act of 1900 put the U.S. solidly on the gold standard.

In 1933, because of the Great Depression, President Franklin D. Roosevelt effectively ended the gold standard in the U.S. when he recalled all gold and silver certificates. (Gold and silver certificates were paper money that could be exchanged for an equal amount of gold or silver.) In addition, the Gold Reserve Act of 1934 set the value of gold at $35 an ounce and ended the coinage of gold. President Nixon cut the ties of U.S. currency to gold when he declared in 1971 that the value of U.S. money would be based on its trading value on the world market.

William Jennings Bryan[2]

After his defeat in the presidential election of 1896, Bryan ran for the same office twice more—in 1900 and 1908. He lost both times. Bryan continued to champion causes of the common people such as the eight-hour workday, a graduated federal income tax and the right for women to vote. President Wilson appointed Bryan his Secretary of State in 1913, but he resigned from that office in 1915 in protest of Wilson's policies towards Germany before World War I.

During the final decade of his life, Bryan was one of the leaders of the conservative Fundamentalist religious movement in the U.S. Because of his religious beliefs, he was on the prosecution team in the so-called Scope's "Monkey Trial" in 1925. John Scopes was accused of teaching Darwin's theory of the evolution of species in his science classes, which was against the law in Tennessee. Although defense attorney Clarence Darrow's cross-examination of Bryan made Bryan look ridiculous during the trial, the prosecution won the case against Scopes. Bryan died less than a week after the trial ended.

[2]*Ibid.*, pp. 113-114.

Introduction to the "Cross of Gold" Speech Questions

1. Did the U.S. begin on the gold system, using bimetallism, or on some other standard for its currency? Give evidence from the text to support your answer. _____

   _____

   _____

2. Explain why wealthy people opposed bimetallism in the 1890s. _____

   _____

   _____

3. a. When and why did the U.S. go off the gold standard? b. What has the value of U.S. currency been based on since 1971? _____

   _____

4. What were four reforms for the common man and woman that Bryan favored? _____

   _____

   _____

   _____

5. What was the highest national office that Bryan held? _____

6. Thought Question: a. What might you conclude was the cause of Bryan's death after reading the last paragraph of his biography? b. What might have been two other causes of his death? _____

   _____

   _____

The "Cross of Gold" Speech[1]

by William Jennings Bryan

And now, my friends, let me come to the paramount issue. If they ask us why it is that we say more on the money question than we say upon the tariff question, I reply that, if protection has slain its thousands, the gold standard has slain its tens of thousands. If they ask us why we do not embody in our platform all the things that we believe in, we reply that when we have restored the money of the Constitution all other necessary reforms will be possible; but that until this is done there is no other reform that can be accomplished.

Now, friends, let me talk about the most important subject. Some critics will ask me why I am talking more about the money issue than about the taxes on imported goods. I will reply to them that import taxes have hurt thousands of people, but the gold standard has hurt tens of thousands of people. The critics will ask us why our political promises don't include all the things we believe in. We will answer that the solution to all of those problems will be possible if we go back to the money policy of the time of the writing of the Constitution. But if we don't go back to the old money system, we cannot make any of the other reforms we need.

Here is the line of battle, and we care not upon which issue they force the fight; we are prepared to meet them on either issue or on both. If they tell us that the gold standard is the standard of civilization, we reply to them that this, the most enlightened of all the nations of the earth, has never declared for a gold standard and that both the great parties this year are declaring against it. If the gold standard is the standard of civilization, why my friends, should we not have it? If they come to meet us on that issue we can present the history of our nation. More than that; we can tell them that they will search the pages of history in vain to find a single instance where the common people of any land have ever declared themselves in favor of the gold standard. They can find where the holders of fixed investments have declared for a gold standard, but not where the masses have.

We draw the line of battle here. We don't care which issue we fight about. We are ready to fight about the gold standard, about the tax on imports or about both issues. They may tell us that the gold standard is the standard of civilization. We will reply that the U.S., the best-informed nation on Earth, never favored a gold standard, and both of its political parties are against the gold standard. If the gold standard is the standard of civilization, then why shouldn't the United States have it? If they argue with us about the gold standard, we can tell them that never in history have the common people said they favored the gold standard. The wealthy people have been in favor of the gold standard, but the masses of people have not.

[1]*The World's Great Orators and Their Orations* by Charles Morris, Philadelphia, Pennsylvania, The John C. Winston, Co., 1902.

Name _____

The "Cross of Gold" Speech

by William Jennings Bryan

Mr. Carlyle said, in 1878, that this was a struggle between "the idle holders of capital" and "the struggling masses who produce the wealth and pay the taxes of the country"; and, my friends, the question we are to decide is: upon which side will the Democratic party fight; upon the side of "the idle holders of idle capital" or upon the side of "the struggling masses?" That is the question which the party must answer first, and then it must be answered by each individual hereafter. The sympathies of the Democratic party, as shown by the platform, are on the side of the struggling masses who have ever been the foundation of the Democratic party. There are two ideas of government. There are those who believe that, if you will only legislate to make the well-to-do prosperous, their prosperity will leak through on those below. The Democratic idea, however, has been that if you legislate to make the masses prosperous, their prosperity will find its way through every class which rests upon them.

Mr. Carlyle (a historian of the 1800s) said that there is a struggle between the wealthy people and the workers who create the wealth and pay the nation's taxes. The question we have to decide for the Democrats is whether the party will be on the side of the wealthy people who don't work or the side of the struggling workers. The Democratic Party must answer that question first. Then the individual members of the party must answer that question. The Democratic Party is sympathetic to the masses. Its promises for this election (its platform) show that. These struggling workers have been the foundation of the Democratic Party. There are two economic theories that the government has. One idea is that you should pass laws that benefit the wealthy, and the money will leak down to those who are not rich. The Democrats, however, have the idea that you make laws to help the poor masses, and all of the classes above them will benefit, too.

You come to us, and tell us, that the great cities are in favor of the gold standard; we reply that the great cities rest upon our broad and fertile prairies. Burn down your cities and leave our farms, and your cities will spring up again as if by magic; but destroy our farms and the grass will grow in the streets of every city in the country.

Other people tell us that the people who live in the cities favor the gold standard. Our reply is that the cities rest on the farms on the prairies. If you burn down the cities but leave the farms, the cities will quickly be rebuilt. If you burn down the farms, however, the cities will soon be destroyed as well.

The "Cross of Gold" Speech

by William Jennings Bryan

My friends, we declare that this nation is able to legislate for its own people on every question, without waiting for the aid or consent of any other nation on earth; and upon that issue we expect to carry every State in the Union. I shall not slander the inhabitants of the fair State of Massachusetts, nor the inhabitants of the State of New York, by saying that, when they are confronted with the proposition, they still declare that this nation is not able to attend to its own business. It is the issue of 1776 over again. Our ancestors, when but three millions in number, had the courage to declare their political independence of every other nation; shall we, their descendants, when we have grown to seventy millions, declare that we are less independent than our forefathers? No, my friends, that will never be the verdict of our people. Therefore, we care not upon what lines that battle is fought. If they say bimetallism is good, but that we cannot have it until other nations help us, we reply that, instead of having a gold standard because England has, we will restore bimetallism, and then let England have bimetallism because the United States has it. If they dare to come out in the open field and defend the gold standard as a good thing, we will fight them to the uttermost. Having behind us the producing masses of this nation and of the world, supported by the commercial interests, the laboring interests, and the toilers everywhere, we will answer their demand for a gold standard by saying to them: You shall not press down upon the brow of labor this crown of thorns; you shall not crucify mankind upon a cross of gold.

The United States is able to pass its own laws without the help or approval of any other nation on Earth. We expect every state in the Union would agree that we are able to make our own laws without any nation's help. We won't lie about Massachusetts or New York and say that they think we can't make our own laws. It is 1776 (the American Revolution) all over again. When our ancestors numbered only three million people in the colonies, they had the courage to declare their independence of all other nations. Now, we number 70 million people. Are we going to be less independent than our ancestors? No, our people will never say that. Therefore, we do not care on what lines the battle is fought. Our critics may say that bimetallism[2] is good but that we can't have it unless other nations have it. Our answer is that rather than go on the gold standard because that is what England has, we should have a bimetal standard and let England follow us and also have a bimetal standard. If they defend the gold standard as a good thing, we will fight them to the end. The workers of the U.S. and the world support us. The commercial interests, laborers and workers everywhere support bimetallism. So we answer the demand for the gold standard with these words: "You shall not put a crown of thorns on the foreheads of laborers; you shall not crucify men on a cross of gold."

---

[2]*Bimetallism* meant the coining of both gold and silver into money. In other words, it meant an economy based on two precious metals—gold and silver—instead of being on the gold standard and coining only gold.

Name _____

The "Cross of Gold" Speech Questions

1. According to Bryan's speech, what were the two most important economic problems of the late 1890s? _____

2. a. What is the definition of *bimetallism*? (See footnote.) b. What is the name of the other economic system that is the opposite of bimetallism? _____

   _____

   _____

3. a. What political party was Bryan addressing in this speech? b. List four groups of people whose economic welfare Bryan is concerned about in this speech. _____

   _____

   _____

4. Apparently, one of the arguments against bimetallism in the U.S. was that England and other foreign nations were on the gold standard. What was Bryan's response to that argument? _____

   _____

5. It was common for speakers and writers of the 19th century to refer to themes and stories from the Bible in their works. Their audiences would have understood these references immediately. These references are one form of literary allusion. What Bible story did Bryan refer to when he mentioned the "crown of thorns" and being crucified on "the cross of gold"? _____

   _____

6. Historical Research Question: What third political party also nominated Bryan for President in 1896 because of the bimetallism issue? _____

7. Extra Credit: What Bible story did Bryan refer to when he said at the beginning of this speech "if protection has slain its thousands, the gold standard has slain its tens of thousands"?

   _____

Internet Research Ideas

1. Biographies
   a. Alexander Hamilton—first Secretary of the Treasury under the Constitution.

   b. Paul Volker—chairman of the Federal Reserve Board in the 1980s.

   c. Alan Greenspan—chairman of the Federal Reserve Board in the 1990s; presided over one of the longest periods of peacetime prosperity in U.S. history.

   d. William Jennings Bryan—campaigned for bimetallism in 1890s; ran for President three times; served as Secretary of State under President Wilson.

   e. Salmon P. Chase—Secretary of the Treasury 1861-64; proposed national banking system established in 1863; helped found Republican Party; Chief Justice of Supreme Court 1864-1873; presided over impeachment trial of President Andrew Johnson.

   f. John Sutter—owner of Sutter's Mill near Sacramento, California, where gold was discovered in 1848; lost all of his cattle and land as gold seekers invaded his property.

   g. Roger B. Taney—Secretary of the Treasury under President Jackson; helped Jackson destroy the 2nd National Bank; Chief Justice of the Supreme Court; especially noted for his pro-slavery decision in the Dred Scott v. Sandford case.

   h. Levi Strauss—made and sold durable denim jeans to miners; his company still makes jeans today; denim trousers sometimes called "Levis."

   i. Winfield Scott Stratton—millionaire who made his fortune in the gold mines of Cripple Creek, Colorado.

   j. Molly Brown—she and her husband became rich from gold mine in Colorado; survived sinking of *Titanic*; Denver socialite; subject of the movie *The Unsinkable Molly Brown*.

   k. General William A. Custer—led the expedition to the Black Hills, South Dakota, that discovered gold; clashed with Sioux as whites invaded the Black Hills in search of gold; killed at Battle of Little Big Horn against the Sioux.

   l. Sitting Bull—one of the leaders of the Sioux in their resistance to white invasion of the Black Hills.

   m. Crazy Horse—one of the leaders of the Sioux in their resistance to white invasion of the Black Hills; helped defeat Custer at Battle of Little Big Horn.

   n. Henry Comstock—discovered silver in Nevada in 1829 in what became the Comstock Lode.

   o. George Hearst—one of those who made millions from the Comstock Lode silver mine; father of William Randolph Hearst, newspaper baron.

   p. Adolph Sutro—engineer who designed and built a three-to-four-mile tunnel for ventilation and drainage in the Comstock mines in the 1870s; one of the greatest engineering feats of the 19th century.

Internet Research Ideas

q. John W. Mackay and William Flood—Irish immigrants who became the so-called "Silver Kings" when they made their fortunes at the Comstock Lode silver mine in Nevada.

r. Samuel L. Clemens—author better known as Mark Twain; journalist and miner in Nevada in his early career; wrote *Roughing It* about his Western experiences.

s. Horace A.W. Tabor—grubstaked two miners in Leadville, Colorado, and earned one million dollars on his investment; built Tabor Grand Opera House in Denver; divorced first wife Augusta to marry Elizabeth "Baby" Doe; acquired fabulous Matchless Mine; went broke.

t. Bret Harte—"local color" author who wrote about the gold fields in such short stories as "The Outcasts of Poker Flat" and "The Luck of Roaring Camp."

u. Albert Gallatin—Secretary of the Treasury from 1801-1814; immigrant from Switzerland to U.S. in 1780; minister to France and Great Britain; deep interest in Native American culture.

2. Gold and Silver Discoveries in the United States

a. Georgia—gold discovered on Cherokee land in 1829; Cherokees driven off the land shortly thereafter.

b. "Pikes Peak or Bust"—Aurora, Colorado; gold discovered near Denver in 1858.

c. California—gold discovered at Sutter's Mill 1848; gold rush in 1849.

d. Black Hills, South Dakota—gold discovered by an expedition led by Colonel William A. Custer in 1874; Sioux forced to give up all claims to the Black Hills in 1876.

e. Klondike, Alaska—gold rush in 1898-1899.

f. Cripple Creek, Colorado—gold discovered in 1890s.

g. Comstock Lode, Nevada—greatest silver mine in U.S. history discovered 1859.

h. Gila City, Arizona—gold discovered in 1853.

i. Wickenburg and Tombstone in Arizona (between 1850 and 1870).

j. Elk City and Oro Fino in Idaho (between 1850 and 1870).

k. Diamond City, Virginia City and Bannack in Montana (between 1850 and 1870).

l. Virginia City and Aurora in Nevada (between 1850 and 1870).

3. U.S. soldiers removed the Cherokees from their lands in Georgia in the winter of 1838-1839 on what became known as the Trail of Tears. Among the causes of this removal were land hunger, the gold rush in Georgia and President Jackson's hostility toward Native Americans. About four thousand of the Cherokees died on the thousand-mile trek to present-day Oklahoma. Research and report on this incident.

4. Miners used several methods of getting gold out of the ground depending on where and in what form it was found. Several students could each research and report on one of these methods: a. panning for gold and/or using a cradle; b. using a sluice including the Long Tom; c. dredging a riverbed and/or diverting the river to mine the bed; d. placer mining (also called hydraulic mining); e. digging tunnels and shafts into a mountain; f. strip mining (used more for coal, iron and copper rather than precious metals).

5. Topics related to mining that might interest some students include: a. safety issues in mines that frequently claimed miners' lives; b. the miners' organization of labor unions to raise pay, reduce hours and improve working conditions; and c. environmental concerns about mining, especially strip mining.

6. Three ways to get from the east coast of the U.S. to the gold mines in California were: a. crossing the Isthmus of Panama before the canal was built, b. sailing 15,000 to 17,000 miles around the tip of South America or c. going overland across the continent using the Mormon or Oregon Trails and taking the California Trail into the gold fields. Three students could each research one of the routes to the gold fields.

7. San Francisco grew at a tremendous rate after gold was discovered in 1848 near present-day Sacramento and in other places in the Sierras. It was a seaport where some of the gold-seekers landed, a town of shops that sold the miners their supplies and finally, the respectable city where the wealthy built their mansions and settled down. Research and report on the history of San Francisco from the gold rush in 1848 to the earthquake and fire of 1906.

Internet Research Ideas

The purpose of this exercise is to give students a better understanding of the U.S. economy and the measures the government uses to track economic expansion and contraction. Interpreting these figures allows the Treasury Department and the Federal Reserve Board to set economic policy.

Put the students in small groups of three people each. You may want to limit the number of economic indicators each group needs to find to four or five topics. Obvious places to search for information on the internet would be *The New York Times, The Washington Post, The Wall Street Journal*, your local newspaper and government publications. (The teacher should probably do some preliminary research so that he or she can quickly lead students to the sources they will need.) Statistics are published quarterly after a time lag during which the figures are collected and interpreted. Where possible, students should indicate whether the economic indicators are up or down compared to the previous quarter or year.

After the students have completed their research, they should report out of their groups. A class recorder should keep a record of the statistics on a chalkboard or other large-scale medium. View all of the figures and discuss with the students whether the economic picture is improving or worsening. Also discuss what the Federal Reserve Board and other government agencies could do to improve the economy. Most often the Federal Reserve Board raises or lowers the prime interest rate. Could Congress pass laws to regulate certain aspects of the economy or institute a tax cut to give consumers more money to spend?

Leading Economic Indicators[1]

Leading economic indicators give economists a way to predict how well the economy will be doing in the future.

1. Average number of hours employees work in manufacturing per week: The more hours they work, the better the economy is doing. If the economy is doing badly, employers usually reduce the number of hours worked before firing workers.

2. Average weekly claims of people applying for unemployment insurance for the first time: The more people who apply for unemployment insurance, the worse the economy is doing.

3. Applications for new building permits for private homes: When the number of applications for building permits is high, people are willing to buy homes. If people are buying homes, it means they are securely employed and the economy is doing well.

4. The prices of the 500 common stocks listed in the Standard and Poor's stock index: Rising prices on the New York Stock Exchange indicate that investors have confidence in the stock market. Confidence in the stock market indicates confidence that the economy in general is doing well.

---

[1]"Economic Indicators"   www.kc.frb.org/fed101/policy/indicators_print.htm

5. <u>Index of consumer expectations:</u> Surveyors collect information about consumer expectations by asking questions in a survey. Expectations influence consumer behavior, and behavior influences the economy. For instance, if consumers expect that their income is going to improve, they might buy a new car, which will improve the economy.

6. <u>Manufacturers' new orders of new consumer goods and materials:</u> Consumer goods are things that people buy such as cars, refrigerators, clothing, furniture and toys. These are different from things that factories buy (machines to make consumer goods) or things that farmers buy (tractors and combines) that are used to make more money. If people are buying more consumer goods, the economy is doing well.

7. <u>Manufacturers' new orders, nondefense capital goods:</u> Capital goods are products that are used to make money such as machines that factories use to make things to sell to the public. Nondefense materials would be things that do not have to do with war, such as dishwashers, cars, cosmetics, furniture and books. If manufacturers' order new capital goods that are not related to war, it means that they are expanding or modernizing their factories in order to produce more goods. If factories are expanding to manufacture more goods, the economy is expanding and doing well, too.

8. <u>Money supply:</u> This is an estimate of how much money is circulating in the economy. The money supply includes actual currency (coins and paper money), money in checking and savings accounts, money invested in the stock market (in mutual funds, for instance) and traveler's checks. In general, more money in circulation means that people have more money to spend and that the economy is doing well. Less money in circulation usually means economic hard times.

Internet Research Ideas

Coincident Economic Indicators

These economic signs tell how the economy is doing right now.

9. Employees on nonagricultural payrolls: This figure is the number of people who have jobs anywhere except on farms and ranches. This includes permanent and temporary employees. The more people who have jobs, the better the economy is doing.

10. Personal income: This figure includes income from all sources such as salaries, hourly wages, tips, returns on stock market investments, royalties, interest on savings accounts, income from a personally owned business and retirement pensions. The higher personal income is (after it is adjusted for inflation), the better the economy is doing.

11. Index of industrial production: This is a measure of the physical output of factories, mines and gas and electric utilities. It includes an actual count of what is produced, an estimate of the value of the products, and a count of the number of people employed in producing these items. The higher the production of goods, raw materials and utilities, the better the economy is doing.

Lagging Economic Indicators

These figures are available after a change in the economy has occurred. They are helpful in predicting how long the good or bad economic situation will last.

12. Average duration of unemployment: This figure shows the average number of weeks that jobless people have been unemployed. The longer people are unemployed, the worse the economy is doing.

13. Consumer installment credit outstanding in relationship to personal income: This figure shows how far in debt the average person is. It would include the amount of credit card debt and payments to stores for things like cars, appliances and furniture. In general, if people are confident enough to increase their debt, then the economy has improved.

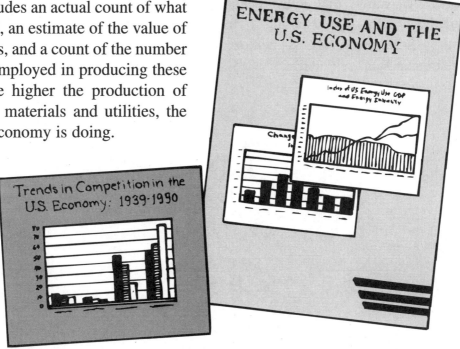

Multiple Intelligence Activities

Verbal/Linguistic Intelligence

1. Use Bret Harte's "The Outcasts of Poker Flat" or "The Luck of Roaring Camp" as oral interpretation pieces. Edit one of the stories so that it fits the time limit; rehearse it privately and perform it for your classmates.

2. Present a mock trial in which John Sutter tries to get payment for his land and cattle that were taken from him by the invading gold hunters at Sutter's Mill, California.

3. Research the situation that led to the Cherokee Removal from their lands in Georgia in the 1830s. Be sure to read up on the Supreme Court decisions on this situation. Two students will be the opposing lawyers who present their arguments to the Supreme Court. Nine students will be Supreme Court justices who ask legal questions of the lawyers. Present this mock trial before the class. At the end of the presentations, the Supreme Court justices make their ruling. (A movie that shows a good model of the process of presenting a case before the Supreme Court is *Gideon's Trumpet* starring Henry Fonda.)

Visual/Spatial Intelligence

1. Research the latest security technology (motion detectors, heat detectors, laser beams, etc.) for protecting valuable objects. Also find out about the strongest materials for building bank vaults, underground bunkers and other protected areas. Then design a building and the appropriate security technology for updating the Gold Vault at Fort Knox.

2. Over a 10-year period, the U.S. is issuing quarters that honor each of the 50 states with special designs appropriate to the history and achievements of each state. Draw a design for your state. (If your state's quarter has already been issued, draw a design different from the one that was officially used.)

3. Study the way the U.S. mint makes coins and/or paper money. Draw a diagram showing the main points of that process. Use the diagram to explain the methods of printing or coining money to your classmates.

Multiple Intelligence Activities

Auditory Intelligence

1. Research General George S. Patton's military career during World War II and write a rap song that describes his exploits.

2. Music from three movies related to the topics in this work might interest students. *The Unsinkable Molly Brown* (a musical about one of the people who made money in a Colorado mining town), *Patton* (a biographical movie about General George S. Patton) and *Goldfinger* (a James Bond movie about an attack on the gold reserves at Fort Knox) all have instrumental or vocal music that students might want to learn and perform for their classmates. (Note: Some parents would find *Patton* and *Goldfinger* unsuitable for their middle school children. Students should get the music from another source rather than watching the movies unless they have their parents' permission to do so.)

3. Some Army cavalry and armored units have theme songs. Research the 15 or so units whose home is Fort Knox; find out if they have theme songs; sing or play one of these themes or a medley of them for your classmates.

Logical/Mathematical Intelligence

1. The value of the U.S. dollar is now measured on the international market against the value of other nations' money. (For instance, one U.S. dollar might be worth 16 Japanese yen.) Follow the international market for a week or longer. Make a chart that shows each day's value of the dollar in relationship to the British euro, the French euro, the German euro, the Russian ruble and the Japanese yen. After completing your chart, make a graph for each foreign currency and plot the rise and fall of the U.S. dollar in relationship to each of the five nations' money.

2. There is also an international market in precious metals. Follow the market for gold and silver for a week or longer. Keep a chart of each day's dollar values for these precious metals. When you have finished your chart, enter that information onto a graph showing the rise and fall of the value of gold and silver over time.

Multiple Intelligence Activities

Body/Kinesthetic Intelligence

1. Choreograph and perform a dance based on one of the historical events that is listed in Internet Research Ideas 1: Biographies.

2. Demonstrate to your classmates the process of panning for gold from a stream.

Interpersonal Intelligence

General Patton was removed from his command and greatly criticized for slapping a soldier that Patton thought was a coward. Read about Patton's character. Find out what qualities made him such an outstanding leader. What flaws in his character probably caused him to slap the soldier? List his strengths and weaknesses as a leader. Then write a short essay in which you explain how Patton used his strengths and overcame his weaknesses to be a successful leader.

Intrapersonal Intelligence

1. Research the Trail of Tears. Pretend you are writing a letter to President Jackson protesting the treatment of the Cherokees as they are removed from their homes in Georgia to the Indian Territory in what is now Oklahoma. Describe the conditions on the Trail of Tears and in Indian Territory as you try to persuade Jackson to change his policy towards the Cherokees and to help them.

2. Pretend that you are a gold or silverseeker during any of the gold or silver rushes mentioned in Internet Research Ideas 1: Biographies. After doing some research on the gold or silver camp you chose, write seven to 10 diary entries in which you describe the conditions in the camp, the hard work involved in mining, the loneliness and dangers at your claim, the high cost of food and the fun times you occasionally have.

Multiple Intelligences

Divide students into groups to do summary projects on Fort Knox. Possible activities would include creating a web site, doing a PowerPoint presentation, writing and scanning photographs for a brochure, making a videotape, writing and recording a radio program or writing and performing a musical.

Answer Key

Fort Knox Bullion Depository Questions, page 7

1. a. The five gold depositories are at Fort Knox, the Philadelphia Mint, the Denver Mint, the West Point Bullion Depository and the San Francisco Assay Office. b. The President of the United States supervises the gold depositories.

2. Bullion is gold or silver in the form of bars or sometimes coins.

3. At $36 per ounce, a gold bar would be worth $14,400. ($36 x 400 ounces = $14,400)

4. A gold bar weighs 33.333… pounds. (400 ounces divided by 12 ounces per pound = 33.333… (The last three dots represent a repeating decimal.)

5. The depository and the vault are made of steel and reinforced concrete.

6. No one knows the entire combination. It takes several people, each of whom knows only part of the combination, to open the safe.

7. There are at least two reasons why the gold is distributed in five places in the U.S. One of them is to protect the U.S. gold supply. If it is located in several places, it is less likely that an attack or natural disaster would destroy the entire gold supply. The second reason is for ease of distribution. If the gold had to be moved for any reason, it would be easier to move it from one of the five depositories that is closest to its final destination.

8. Fort Knox was built during President Franklin Roosevelt's administration.

Major General Henry Knox Questions, page 10

1. Knox's parents came from Ireland.

2. After his father died, Knox became a clerk in a bookstore.

3. Knox got the cannons from Fort Ticonderoga, Vermont, and dragged them on ox sleds all the way to Boston, Massachusetts.

4.

WON	LOST
Boston, MA	New York, NY
(not actually a battle)	Brandywine, PA
Trenton, NJ	Germantown, PA
Princeton, NJ	
Yorktown, VA	

5. Washington appointed Knox as his Secretary of War because Knox was an experienced and knowledgeable artilleryman and because Knox was his friend.

6. Knox was better at the use of artillery in warfare than at business because different people have different talents. Apparently, Knox also liked artillery better than business because he read about the former from an early age. Answers will vary. Give credit for logical answers.

Answer Key

Fort Knox Military Installation Questions, page 13

1. World War I caused the U.S. government to buy the land that became Fort Knox.

2. The government built the U.S. Bullion Depository at Fort Knox in 1936-1937.

3. The main job of the military installation at Fort Knox is training soldiers in the use of armored vehicles in combat.

4. a. Army cavalry units ride in tanks now.

   b. Armored divisions ride in armored vehicles.

5. Fort Knox was closed in 1922 because of the reduction in military forces that followed the end of World War I.

6. Fort Knox was re-opened in the 1930s because the U.S. Bullion Depository was built there and because the 7th Cavalry Brigade went there to help the citizens who were flooded out of Louisville, Kentucky.

7. England and some other foreign nations stored their valuables at Fort Knox during World War II either because they were being bombed by the Germans or were occupied by German troops.

8. Kentucky was a border state during the Civil War; it remained in the Union, but its southern border was also part of the border between the United States and the Confederate States. That meant that each side would have tried to send troops through Kentucky in order to attack its enemy on the other side of the border.

Fort Knox—Reading a Chart, pages 14-15

1. a. The chart shows information about Expenditures, Active Duty Personnel and Civilian Employees.

   b. The new fiscal year begins on October 1.

   c. Fort Knox spent $458,571,000 in 1984.

   d. i. The information on the chart is from *Atlas/Data Abstract for the United States and Selected Areas* that is published by the Department of Defense.

   ii. It is important to know the source of information in order to judge its accuracy.

   e. i. Payroll includes retirement pay.

   ii. No, there is no column on the chart that shows the number of retirees on the payroll.

   f. Active Duty Personnel are those who are enlisted in the military, while civilians are people who are not in the military.

   g. *DOD* stands for Department of Defense.

   h. The chart shows financial information for the years 1984 through 1998.

2. The Navy first hired civilians at Fort Knox in1992.

3. a. Fort Knox spent $16,138,000 more in 1991 than it did in 1992. ($630,741,000 − $614,603,000 = $16,138,000.)

   b. The amount of money paid for Prime Contracts was reduced from $108,409,000 in 1991 to $93,412,000 in 1992

Answer Key

c. One would expect that the number of total personnel would have been reduced also to account for the savings in total money spent. This hypothesis is true. The total number of personnel working at Fort Knox in 1991 was 17,661, while in 1992 it was only 16,607.

4. The average number of Air Force Personnel employed from 1984 through 1998 was 4/5 of a person. (12 people divided by 15 years = 4/5 of a person.)

5. a. The highest amount spent on Prime Contracts was $144,262,000 in 1996.

   b. The amount spent on Prime Contracts would vary depending on the projects going on at Fort Knox such as building new facilities.

6. a. The military men and women would spend some of their pay in the nearest city for food, civilian clothing, entertainment and possibly housing.

   b. Civilian employees would earn their money from the government and spend almost all of it in the city near the base where they lived.

Patton Museum of Cavalry and Armor Questions, page 18

1. Patton had to change his concept of what cavalry meant during World War I.

2. Three examples that show that Patton was successful in using tanks and armored vehicles in battle were his (and his Allies) defeat of Rommel's Afrika Korps in North Africa, his conquest of Sicily and his relief of the besieged city of Bastogne during World War II. (Students only need two correct answers.)

3. The Patton Museum of Cavalry and Armor at Fort Knox was probably named for General Patton because of his famous successes in using armored vehicles against the Germans during World War II.

4. Visitors to the museum have to have photo I.D.s in order to enter the base and cannot be carrying any weapons.

5. Four types of armored vehicles include tanks, armored cars and trucks, self-propelled guns and LSTs (Landing Ship, Tanks).

6. Among the reasons people might visit the Patton Museum of Cavalry and Armor are the following: they are interested in history; they are writing a book and doing research on armored vehicles; they were in the military and want to revisit equipment they used in the past; they are war gamers and want to see the real equipment; or they are interested in military technology.

Answer Key

Alexander Hamilton—First Secretary of the Treasury Questions, page 21

1. The three sources of debt were money loaned to the national government by its citizens, money loaned to the national government by foreign countries and the states' debts.

2. The three sources of income were an import tax, an excise tax and miscellaneous fees and taxes.

3. It was important to pay off the national debt so that citizens would continue to buy government bonds and foreign nations would loan the U.S. money again should we need it.

4. Hamilton thought it was right for the national government to pay off the states' debts because they had incurred these debts while fighting the Revolutionary War, and the whole nation had benefited from winning its independence. He also wanted to gain the loyalty of the debt-ridden states to the new national government, and he could do that by relieving them of their debts.

5. Hamilton's compromise in the Assumption Bill was to pay off the largely Northern states' debts and place the new national capital, Washington, D.C., in the South.

6. a. The major argument against the National Bank was that it was not specifically allowed by the Constitution.

   b. Hamilton's major argument for the National Bank was that the "necessary and proper" (or elastic) clause of the Constitution provided for things like the Bank that were necessary for Congress to carry out its other specifically enumerated duties.

7. The National Bank would benefit the U.S. and its citizens by loaning money to businesses and states, providing income to the U.S. through interest on loans, and keeping money in circulation, which would strengthen the nation's economy. In addition, private citizens could earn additional income by investing money in the Bank and earning interest on their investment.

8. a. A quarter is 1/4 of a dollar.

   b. A quarter is 25% of a dollar.

   c. As a decimal, a quarter is .25 of the value of a dollar.

9. Answers will vary. Give credit for those answers that show good use of historical facts and logic.

A History of the United States' Banking System Questions, page 26

1. The name of the first national banking institution was the First Bank of the United States.

2. The three worst depressions shown on this time line were in 1893, 1907 and the 1930s.

3. The longest period of peacetime economic expansion occurred in the 1990s.

4. Paul Volker was a successful chairman of the Federal Reserve Board. His policies brought inflation under control in the 1980s (and might be said to have set the stage for the economic expansion of the 1990s).

5. The only effort to control national banking between 1836 and 1913 was the 1863 National Banking Act that created nationally chartered banks.

Answer Key

6. In general, the period between 1913 and 1954 shows greater efforts by the national government to control the economy. Some examples include the creation of the Federal Reserve Banks in 1914, the Banking Act of 1933 (Glass-Steagall Act), the creation of the Federal Deposit Insurance Corporation in 1933, the U.S.'s going off the gold standard in 1933 and the creation of the Securities and Exchange Commission in 1934.

Introduction to the "Cross of Gold" Speech Questions, page 29

1. The U.S. began its monetary system by using bimetallism. The text says, "The U.S. in 1792 began on a system based on both silver and gold."

2. Wealthy people opposed bimetallism in the 1890s because it would cause inflation that would decrease the value of the money in which they were repaid for the loans they had given other people.

3. a. The U.S. went off the gold standard in 1933 when President Roosevelt recalled all gold and silver certificates. The reason the U.S. went off the gold standard was because of the Great Depression.

   b. Since 1971, the value of U.S. currency has been based on its trading value in the world market.

4. The four reforms Bryan favored included the coining of silver (bimetallism), an eight-hour workday, a graduated federal income tax and women's right to vote.

5. The highest office Bryan held was Secretary of State under President Wilson.

6. a. One might conclude that Bryan died because he was ridiculed by the defense in the Scope's "Monkey Trial" which had concluded just days earlier.

   b. Bryan might have died of old age. (He was 65 at a time when the human life span was shorter than it is now.) He also might have died of an illness that had gone unnoticed and undiagnosed until his death.

The "Cross of Gold" Speech Questions, page 33

1. Bryan says that the two most important economic issues of the day are the "money question" (bimetallism) and "the tariff question" (import taxes).

2. a. Bimetallism is the coining of both gold and silver into money.

   b. The opposite of *bimetallism* is the gold standard.

3. Bryan's "Cross of Gold" speech was addressed to the Democratic Party. b. Bryan spoke in favor of the "common man"; "the masses";"the struggling masses who produce the wealth and pay the taxes of the country"; farmers of the "broad and fertile prairies"; the "producing masses"; "the commercial interests, the laboring interests and the toilers everywhere" and "labor."

4. Bryan's response was that the U.S. should take the lead in being a country with bimetallism and let England catch up by changing its system to bimetallism, too.

Answer Key

5. Bryan was referring to the crucifixion of Jesus and the events leading up to His crucifixion.

6. The Populist Party also nominated Bryan to run for President in 1896.

7. Bryan was referring to the story of David and King Saul after David had killed Goliath and became part of King Saul's court. When the two came back from battle, the crowds sang that Saul had killed his thousands, but that David had killed his tens of thousands. This incident increased King Saul's hatred of David.